Song
Of
Creation

Poems by Greg P. Thompson

Order this book online at www.trafford.com
or email orders@trafford.com

Most Trafford titles are also available at major online book retailers.

Printed in Victoria, BC, Canada.

ISBN: 978-1-4269-1842-1 (sc)
ISBN: 978-1-4269-1843-8 (hc)

Library of Congress Control Number: 2009937628

*Our mission is to efficiently provide the world's finest, most comprehensive book publishing
service, enabling every author to experience success. To find out how to publish your book, your
way, and have it available worldwide, visit us online at www.trafford.com*

Trafford rev. 12/23/09

Trafford
PUBLISHING® www.trafford.com North America & international
toll-free: 1 888 232 4444 (USA & Canada)
phone: 250 383 6864 ♦ fax: 812 355 4082

Table of Contents

PREFACE

Dear Friend,

All creation and all of life, every aspect of it, sing a song. Some songs are glad, some sad. All invite us to meet the Singer! May you find Him in these pages.

Dedicated:

First, to Deb, loving and lovely wife of thirty-five years, whose life is one great epic song-poem of endurance and grace.

Then, to all friends and family members whose lives and love have contributed (sometimes specifically) to the poetry contained in this volume.

Lastly (but of first importance) to the One who gives a song to sing every day. ***Soli Deo Gloria***

Greg P. Thompson

Poet's Prayer

Like Whitman let me wax prosaic,
Effusive, from a large magnanimous heart.
Like Shakespeare, may I sense and share
The glories and guffaws of men,
The beauty and rhythm of love,
And reverence masked in earthy imagery-
All done in iambic pentameter.
Ah, that I like Hopkins may swift-soar
On brilliant phrase and striking metaphor,
Or with A. Pope master the rhyming couplet
That lends a seeker entrance to the craft.
Like Dickenson make me apt
To hold the strong mind rapt with attention,
To struggle to dig deeply for her gold.
With Wordsworth, keep me in the dance
Of creation and creativity,
And never let me lose bright nature's song.
Sir, how I long,
Like David, to laud in parallel praises
Heaven's high King.

Chapter 1

Song of Creation

Angel Said to the Puppy Dog

Angel said to the puppy dog,
"Listen to the earth."
Sat them both on a hollow log,
Eastern sun shone fiery girth.
Puppy held a studied pose,
Panted, I think he grinned-
Ears and sharp eyes, twitching nose
Moved with every wisp of wind.
Critters are so keen, instinctive,
Close to nature, apt to listen.
Humans civil, yet restrictive;
Ours, the duller intuition.
Could I gain this competence
Of animal's commanding.
Would I had his sharper sense
To match my understanding.

Wasteland

Between my distant point of origin
And destination, welcome travel goal,
Here lies this large unspeakable wasteland-
A paradox of barrenness and beauty.

Some have approached this desert and turned back
And some took stock, braved harshness, and trod on.
Awake, my senses, listen, learn and see
That crossing wasteland is not wasted time!

Here, sun-rays do rare things, not elsewhere seen-
Conspiracies of light and shadow cast
On crags and wind-scarred canyons, grand designs
Where lethal cliffs and spires like castles loom.

The past has brought me here, and futures wait.
If I shall soon recall this arid place
And recognize its stark significance,
Then I embrace it now, while passing through.

Sculptor in Snow

As I drive up the pass on a late autumn day,
The Sculptor invites me to view His display -
Grand abstract treasures, all done in soft white
In fresh-fallen powder the previous night.
Each ridge and each ripple, unique in its kind
Came forth from the depths of His creative mind.
His vision is cosmic, yet lacks no detail;
The strokes are embellished with tracks on the trail.
Fresh snow is His medium, the winds are His tools,
The precious raw goods from the realm which He rules.
His gallery, earth; the art, briefly consigned;
Soon forms will be changing, so now is the time
To take it in gladly, with reverent eye,
To enter and wonder, to ponder and pray
And offer this life as a lump in His hand.
"Great Artist, please fashion a reflective man."

Whispering Woods

Whispering Mississippi woods
Sanction my reflective moods,
Whispering her name.

Whispering oaks and knotty pine
Intimate what joy is mine,
Whispering my name.

Whispering, tall and pathless grove
Hints of deep and mystic love,
Whispering His name.

Song of Creation

On a gray
Ocean day,
Dolphins' sheen
Showed to me
Truest hues
Of the sea.

Bright autumn leaves
Strewn along paths
Of fall forests
Were not, to me,
Out of their place
Or untidy.

Winged Canadians
Flying in a 'V'
Low in wintry sky
Clarified for me
Supernal pattern
Of community.

Servants of the Sun

Look at them! Throngs of them!
Larger, smaller groups of them!
Upright minions, all of them
Worshiping the Sun.

Teeming, fresh with life each day,
Draw it from each morning ray.
Errant few may look away;
Most face the Sun.

Standing with uplifted faces,
Some alone, they take their places,
Bright with winsome, flowing graces-
Servants of the Sun.

Even on the cloudy days,
Seeking its elusive rays,
Trusting its elliptic ways -
When will come the Sun?

Buffeted by wind and rain,
Battered, beaten but not slain,
Drooping, but to rise again,
Rise and face the Sun.

Tall, above a weedy maze,
Longing, with expectant gaze,
Sensing, through a fickle haze
Movements of the Sun.

He climbs high in eastern sky,
They throw kisses in reply.
Such sameness! Now I fathom why...

Offspring of the Sun.

Song of the Blue Whale

You must slow down to hear this song; it lasts
throughout the day.
Do not decline to wait so long; the whale has m
to say.
He takes the rolling emerald stage in concert w
his peers
And labors to rehearse the treasured tune of
countless years.
He trumpets with a measured cadence longing
melodies;
They linger on the salty air like mystic reveries.
What are the lyrics and the message of his anci
song?
It may surprise you once to learn that you have
read him wrong.
Joyful notes to his Creator, sung with manly mi
Instinctive four-part harmony with ocean, sky a
earth,
A song of sympathetic pains, with all of nature
groaning;
He sadly rues the hidden chains, the sin of Ad;
owning.
He would not have you place him higher than h
natural station.
He is content to point us to the Lord of all
creation.
Could he speak our dialect, he would not boast
unity.
"There is not one earth ancestor; the same stro
Hands made you and me!"
How does one show due respect for such an
anthem, clear and strong?
Tremble! Worship and reflect! And humbly sin
along.

The Kite – A Musing

The cord that keeps the kite aloft
Is made of many strands.
Cut the strands and so the cord;
Kite crashes as it lands.
Find in playful paradox
A principle profound:
Like the kite, we soar most freely
Tethered to the ground.

The tail that keeps the kite on course
Looks common to the eye,
Yet with no stabilizing force
Kite wallows in the sky.
Obvious observation
Brings a question to the mind:
What is the cord or knotted tail
That keeps you in the wind?

The breeze that gives the kite its life
Is horrible, yet pure-
Unseen and unpredictable;
It has a signature.
Ponder such analogies
And what they do imply-
Who is the mystifying gale
Who beckons you to fly?

Ocean Rollers

Blue or green waves assault the contoured coast
With layer upon layer of bubbly glaze.
Tides rise and fall, predictable as moon-cycles.
The day and night surf-soundings steady nerves.

The cynic pelican glides along the roller
Like barber's blade along his leather strop,
With sleek, impeccable close tolerance
That just belies the gangling, comic bird.

Deliberate, incessant, watch them come
Like giant whales, the mammoth water mounds.
My ears and eager eyes anticipate -
The forms expand and swell as they approach.

They gather sand and seaweed before breaking,
They peak and churn, then curl and gently burst
In one bright splash of oxygenated foam
Snow-white upon the rocks or printed beach.

Were I to walk ten thousand varied shores
I would not weary of this placid view.
A seeker from the great high landlocked state,
I pause, then gladly start the journey home.

Microcosm

Nature in the microcosm-what does it reveal?
Creation's infinitesimal scale-what is its appeal?
The smaller you decide go, the more you magnify,
More mini-marvels open up to your inquiring eye.
Bee imbibes sweet nectar, morning glimmers with fresh dew.
Spider traps ill-fated fly, long struggle does ensue.
Atom teems with energy as particles revolve.
Raindrop hits the watershed and east or west will move.
Pain and power, life and death, and what was blessed and cursed;
It parallels the larger scale in which we are well versed.
Worlds of minutia wait for those who will inspect.
Joy of new discovery bids you pause, observe, reflect.
We can learn life lessons from things gloriously small;
They teach us of our Maker, Who is glorified in all.

Come the Spring

The red upon the blackbird's wing-
Most luminescent in the spring.
So soft the tepid breezes blow,
So swiftly melts the April snow.
Frogs, foxes, fowl, with noise awake
As run-off fills the urban lake.
Anon, striped bass will fan and dredge
To nest their eggs at water's edge.
The dogs on leash tug, toil and bend
And point their noses to the wind.
Sequestered hearts break free and sing-
Most luminescent, come the spring.

Forest Fever

[with apologies to John Masefield]

I must go into the woods again, to the aspens, ferns and
pines.
And all I ask is a pair of boots – to the path my heart
inclines.
And the hiker's pace, and the trail's rut, and the rose
hips creeping,
And the wise-weathered evergreens, and the bright sun
peeping.

I must go into the woods again, for the lure of the
mountain life
Is a stream lure and a lake lure, and a summons from
city strife.
And all I ask is an autumn breeze that cools me as I go,
Where bright leaves fall and spatter the lane like fire
down below.

I must go into the woods again; close to the earth I am
wooed,
Where the lark sings and the monks chip as they gather
their winter food.
And all I ask is a subtle brush from a keen-eyed canine
friend
And to love the track and to walk the way
And to follow it all to the end.

To the Hiker

Welcome to the outdoors I made for you
I'm glad you came to balance work with play
I'm pleased you came to recreate today.
You made this trail go through my choicest woods-
It is all right; come, walk with me awhile.

Sense my presence,
Feel my pleasure.

Are you in awe of such variety?
I've lined this path with flora just for you,
Dotted these hills with fauna, all for you.
Wait till you see the plans I've laid for you!
You understand the price I paid for you?

Adore my work,
Inhale my breath.

Then go back to the city where you live,
Give thanks, remember, seek and serve me there.

To My Friend, an Evolutionist

How can the same vast ocean
Call forth from you and me
Such vastly different responses?
How can the broad, green tree
Yield contrary conclusions?

How can the same night sky
Give different reasons to dance?
We both gaze in awe and wonder.
But was it design, or chance?
Is that intelligence knowable?

We must admit that bias
Affects our varying views.
But reason is founded on faith;
Whether natural or spiritual, the clues
May be read different ways.

Let us evolve a tolerance,
Create an open exchange.
Truth, our common quest,
Discussion a fair interchange
And friendship our companion on the way.

Chapter 2

Revelation, Reflection and Response

Star Maker

[To the tune, "Spirit" by John Denver]

The Spirit moved and He was born
Two thousand years ago
(When Saturn's rings and Jupiter
Were lined up in a row).
To show His grace, to conquer Hell,
To do the Father's will,
To rule the wind, to teach its song,
And empty hearts to fill.

"Apollo I taught how to rhyme,
Orpheus learned how to play.
Andromeda carries my sign
And I light Vega's way."

Star signs in the galaxy,
An entrance into time;
Lyra got her harp from Him,
Accompanied His climb.
A winter's journey from the tomb
To reach the Father's throne,
To rise again, to sing for you
A song that was unknown.

"Apollo I taught how to rhyme,
Orpheus learned how to play.
Andromeda carries my sign
And I light Vega's way."

Oh God, Your Glory

Oh God, your glory, vast within my view-
The windswept prairie, peaks and endless sky!
Though scarred from Adam's impress, still they glow,
Engaging open mind or searching eye.

Oh God, your glory, hostage in my heart-
Great panoramic pallet of your grace!
Though marred from Adam's impress, still you 'scape
Yourself, transforming this uplifted face.

Oh God, your glory, loose upon my lips-
So timidly I speak to make it known!
Once mute from Adam's impress, now unbound,
I celebrate your glory, now my own.

I Run To My Rest

Jesus said, "Come unto Me, and I will give you rest."
End of all heart journeys, I have found His presence best.
Tempted, tossed tempestuously, buffeted about,
I simply run into my Rest and cast my anchor out.

Christ is a haven of sweet peace, a tranquil resting place
Where sorely tried and troubled hearts are remedied by
Grace.
This is no mindless leisure, nor a wasted idle spree,
But mystical belonging to the One who fashioned me.

When I rest in Him I cease to strive, start to perceive
The depths of One Whose death brought life and
caused me to believe.
Do seek the Son a little while, put tasting to the test;
Most restful of all blessings, most blessed of all rest.

Smiled Kindly on Me

Strolling down the market aisle, a cherub fresh with
youth
Smiled kindly on me, blessed my day, brought home to
me this truth:
A simple smile is a snapshot, captured point in time,
Archived in mind's memory; it lit her eyes, now mine.
A synergy of facial features blossomed into art,
She shot a diplomatic message straight into my heart.
All trust, acceptance, innocence, no judgment and no
guile,
No vices, only virtues were betrayed by such a smile.
Could I see this child again, and may our paths be
crossed,
I would speak a message learned from seeing virtue lost:
"Come harsh adulthood, heavy burdens, life's long,
weary mile,
Never lose the callow joy that fathered forth that
smile!"

Holy Savior

[To the tune "Pocahontas" by Neil Young]

A turning point in history, and Mankind's darkest night;
He suffered Heaven's silence, all His friends had taken
flight
From the garden, to the crowded street;
Soon the cruel nails pierced His hands and feet.

Imagine seeing Peter at the courtyard by the fire,
Confronted by accusers as a coward and a liar.
What would I have done, were I in his shoes?
Dismal failure, able not to choose.

They crucified the King of Kings and they cut the
Master down.
Some soldiers picked His royal robe up from off the
ground,
Shouted insults at the Holy one
As the night fell on the midday sun.

What if I would have been there, gazing into Jesus' face?
Would I have been the scoffer, or the one who begged
for grace
From Messiah, suffering for my sin?
Lord of Heaven, let me enter in.

But you and I did travel on that tragic dying day.
He took our guilt upon himself and He bled it all away,
Died a sinner's death, rose to make us free,
The disciples, you my brother and me.
The disciples, you my sister and me.
Holy Savior!

The Divine Capacity

Take all your evils, thought or done,
Your wrongs, mistakes and sufferings -
Add them over one life span.

Multiply the ample sum
By all who ever lived or shall.
Behold the product if you can!

The whole of sin and consequence
Of Adam's errant daughters, sons,
Lay heavy on the Son of Man.

And who can measure what He bore?
Incalculable! Only God
Could figure such a daring plan.

Emancipation

My Master disenfranchised
The woeful moral tyranny;
He broke the bondage and delivered me.
And trusting Him, dear friend you shall, like me
Be then, thenceforward and forever, free.

In Him

Longing? Pant for Him.
Lustful? Lust for Him.
Running? Run to Him.
Lonely? Long for Him.
Searching? Search for Him.
Finding? Found in Him.
Doubting? Trust in Him.
Desperate? Hope for Him.
Desirous? Desire Him.
Waiting? Wait for Him.
Hungry? Taste of Him.
Thirsty? Drink from Him.
Winning? But for Him.
Losing? Look to Him.
Loving? Love from Him.
Fearful? Fear Him.
Sinning? Cleansed by Him!
Weary? Rest in Him.

In a Friday night home fellowship group, we were discussing the gospel parables. Jesus said, "Listen to this! Behold, the sower went out to sow…" and the seed fell on different soils, representing differing responses to the message of God's kingdom. Gwen, a group member, observed that these different effects could describe any of us, in the attitude of our hearts toward God at different times. This insight resonated personally and prompted the poem, "My Heart is Soil." Many poems come in this way, perhaps occasioned by someone's comment, or hearing an interesting phrase that strikes a poetic chord.

My Heart is Soil

My heart is hard-packed soil,
Dry, cracked and ugly, unresponsive still.
Is there no one to break
This desert ground, to rake and till?
Sun-parched, I want for softening, soothing rain.

My heart is rocky soil;
Emotional appeal scorching, stealing;
I have deceived myself.
No depth, only this shallow feeling.
Sun-blanched, I wither in the mid-day heat.

My heart is thorn-choked soil,
Neglected, overgrown, nor pruned nor picked;
High time for slash and burn!
Sore pressed by cares and conscience pricked;
I cannot see the Son, nor feel His warmth.

My heart is fertile soil!
Warm, welcoming, accepting Spirit-seed,
Sprouting and springing, bringing
What I desired and God decreed;
Sun-drenched, rain-quenched, I dance in the downpour.

Nativity Story

See
And marvel at the mystery
Where truth and myth converge
Like the conjoining of celestial lights.
Behold, two prophecies -
Of the birth of One
And the death of many.
How could they have known?
The timing and the terror of it all!
See
The pagan priests plod west,
Once pagan priests now bowed
Before the Sign they sought (Pagan no more).
See the gifts they bring -
Bright gold for a king,
Incense for a great high priest,
Myrrh to represent the sacrifice to come.
(Would my meager gift signify so much?)
Tremble
As two kings clash,
Madman and Messiah; one a little child,
And one hell-bent to prosper at the cost
of little children's' lives.
Lamentation, weeping and great mourning-
Rachael weeping for her children.
They died in His place, in time.
He will die in theirs, for eternity.
See
Tyranny and tenderness, humility and hope.
Scepter, sword and swaddling clothes

All intertwined into one grand story,
Redemption played on quaint pastoral stage,
Ever told to untold millions,
Never truer than today.
Marvel and be changed
And tell the old, old story once again.

Lights in Old Town

So many lights in Old Town have gone out.
Many have dimmed, a few still brightly burn.
They did not notice the gradual turn.
The older generators are defunct;
They fail to supply the needed power.
And yet the old town dwellers plod along,
Or at least muddle through from day to day.
There's a new and different parish being built
Across a changed river.
The grand and stately Old Town Bridge still stands,
But spans dry sandy bed – the river moved.
There is a bright new bridge now rising up
To span the new and growing, widening river.
There, fresh new opportunities await,
New ways of reaching, building and relating
Some models re-invented, some pre-dating.
We fondly view the remnants of Old Town;
They can't rebuild on cracked, sinking platforms.
Some will not make the crossing to the new.
We wish them well, but also wish they'd come.

Life Was a Gift

Time was a gift;
And with it, gifts to serve, and lessons learned.
Love was a gift;
I gave it all away and it returned.
Life was a gift;
I lived it each new day; the passion burned.
Grace was a gift;
Naught for it but to ever thank the Giver.

Cup of Joy

This day, drink joy from the great Fount of Joy.
Do not be rapt by happiness or pain.
They are like mists along a tree lined path;
Fog comes and goes, but woods and flowers remain.

Raise high the sparkling cup of offered Joy;
See light reflected and refracted there.
It glitters and it dances as it plays
Upon your inner soul, your every care.

Then lower the brimming cup, press to your lips,
Drink deeply, say a prayer, let it refill.
Whatever else may come, take Joy with all.
Want nothing less or more – this is God's will.

Psalm 23 Paraphrase

The Lord is my Muse; I shall not lack inspiration.
He causes me to contemplate a world of metaphors.
He graces my meditation with paradox and poetry.
By His presence am renewed.
He bids me write what will bless others and point them to Him.
As I get older my verse becomes less fanciful and more purposeful.
Because You live within me, the tools of my small craft
are an extension of Your creative genius.
No matter the circumstances, there is a banquet of rhythm, meter,
convention and nuance from which to choose.
Thoughts of You and your work prompt in me
a spontaneous overflow of powerful feeling.
What time I have left is a loving stewardship from You;
And my eternity will be one long and glorious epic only You can
tell.

Said Gnosis to Sophia

σοφια γνωσις σοφια γνωσις σοφια γνωσις σοφια

Proverbs 1:20-22
Eph. 5:13, 14
I Tim. 6:16
John 14:6
Heb. 11:6
Col. 2:3
Said Gnosis to Sophia as they stood
Together on a dim-lit thoroughfare
Where many heard the speech, but few did care:
"My sister, from whence came we, and why here?"
Said she, "We hail from yonder hidden cave,
Our message to proclaim, and some to save."
Sophia said to Gnosis, "Some will follow
So deep within the mighty Rock where lay
All treasures of the Life, the Truth, the Way.
"We siblings are but children of one Father,
The One who dwells in unapproach'ed light -
Transcendent, yet by some well-known aright."
Said Gnosis to Sophia, "Sister, why
Do people wander out along the way?
They stumble, bare and breathless, blind to day."
Said she, "They seek, not knowing where we point-
To understand they seek, not us, but Him.
So few will learn that we are found in Him.
"If they will set heart-sights, however dim
Upon us, we will lead them in the way.
And seeking, they shall find the Light of day."
And some few stood nearby, listened and learned
As hand in hand the siblings walked away –
And some commenced their journey to the Day.
Col. 2:3
Heb. 11:6
John 14:6
I Tim. 6:16
Eph. 5:13, 14
Proverbs 1:20-22

σοφια γνωσις σοφια γνωσις σοφια γνωσις σοφια

All Beauty Beckons You

Reflection of youth in a grandfather's eye,
Moon chasing Orion across the night sky,
Classical notes from a High School band,
Impulse of joy, touch of a hand,
Hope amidst crisis, peace mixed with pain,
Tearful reunion of loved ones again.
Snapshots of beauty on heavenly wings,
Sent by the Maker of beautiful things.
Capture these glimpses of beauty and light.
Open yourself to each touch, sound and sight.
Hear the Name whispered in solitude's place.
Ponder the limitless means of His grace.
Breathe the fresh fragrance of flowers in a wood.
Taste and see that the Lord is good.
Feel a burden by singing made light.
Eye the horizon when sun sets at night.
All beauty beckons you, begs you to see,
Every occurrence is part of a plea,
Warm invitation sent down from above:
Come near the Creator and home to His love.

Shadow Cast

Apex
of all
history,
Pivot
point
of time;
Death of the Redeemer - Cross of heinous crime
Tree that cast its shadow down through history.
Chang-
ing
human
land-
scape,
People
groups,
and me.
Artist
uses
lights
and
shades,
shadows
for effect.
Sinister,
the rugged
cross-
Saving,
the effect!
Lord of all, cleanse all my sin, Stay me through
The strife; Savoir! Cast your shadow 'cross
The
land-
scape
of my
life

Tribulation Saints

Oh, let us worship, let's adore
The God of those who came before –
The tribulation saints
Whose faith looked forward, lived no more
In fear of trials, temptings sore
But fought hard battles, holy war,
What holy countenance they wore -
Worth more than the world.
Many-martyred for His sake,
They bid us follow in their wake
To trust the Savior, not forsake.
And so they were, the tribulation saints.

Oh, let us not be slack to pray
For sisters, brothers in harm's way –
The tribulation saints!
Though cracked from strain, strong pots of clay,
Hold tension and severity.
In many manners we, like they,
His suffering servants, yet today,
Even in a modern world.
They daily fall on calloused knees,
Vanquish the demon when they seize
Upon the Power from which he flees.
And so they are, the tribulation saints.

Oh, to be absent from that band
Who face th'emerging evil hand –
The tribulation saints!
How they will wither, yet withstand
Perplexities in every land,
To persevere and understand
And trust in spite of seeming strand -
Love heaven more than world.
Then, no more sorrow, grief or thirst,
Rejoicing that they braved the worst,
They see the coming kingdom burst
Upon a weary world.
Then victors throng earth's Heaven-throne
In blood-dipped white robes, all their own
And celebrant joy, as yet unknown.
And so we are, the tribulation saints.

[Inspired by the <u>Left Behind</u> series, written by Tim LaHaye and Jerry Jenkins]

agnosto theo

Most real presence, I would see
As seeing solid shapes beyond the mists.
I catch a sparkling glint and sense
A resonating chord struck through mean things.
About me all is ordered, not random –
The windswept prairie, peaks and endless sky.
You shine in spite of forces that would shield.
You boldly break through falsehood fortresses,
Or walls that would but cannot hold you back.
I am alone, searching and wandering, lost,
But I would see; I long to feel and know.
What is this yearning, smoldering in my heart?
I read the ancients' words and spot you there,
Most playful, mythic, patient, powerful-
Great stately Lion with a twitching tail,
As if there were a twinkle in your eye.
Could I but break away pagan pretense
To see that someone, gleaming, beaming there.
Or could there be a fuller revelation,
A clear expression, one to bridge the gap?
Show me, tell me, send someone to reach me!
And I would see and know and follow on.

Chapter 3

Family Portrait

My Mind Races Back

My mind races back To Wah Keeney Park,
And Bergan Peak in the distance, where we would hike
and camp. Mom could see our campfire from the house
and probably said a glad prayer.
I go back to pristine winter days –
And sledding down that hill with the Stunkel boys,
And hot chocolate and cheese toast,
Warming up on the large flagstone hearth
In front of that great quartz rock fireplace.
I race back to the days with Patty, Glenn and Joel,
Growing up next to the Murray kids –
 trouble from the get-go.
And the Jones's across the street –
what were those girls' names?
We rode bikes, threw rocks, skated on the lake,
Caught snakes and played hide and seek at night
And had no money and not a care.
Dad would play that old piano – his rhythm was off.
Mom learned to play the hymns;
They echo still and my mind races back
To her ironing board, the smell of clothes heated and
pressed and Mozart on the radio.
I race back to those days,
When each Christmas was magical,
Even the ones with no gifts under the tree-
The magic increases with years' passage.
My mind races back
To dogs and cats, and unemployment,
To Patty's car wreck and her stilted walk
Down graduation aisle to loud applause,
Hurt but alive – now that's a memory.
My heart races back to the little church,
And pastor Dean, so young, so soon taken!
And in it all, the unseen Hand.

Lines in Garrett's Gift Bible

Dear son, our pride and precious joy,
We call you man, no longer boy,
Fear the testing you now face,
Commend you to the God of grace.
His plans for you are settled sure
Beyond the military corps.
Lift your head up, fight through pain;
Spirits soon will rise again.
This little book contains large truth
Abiding with you from your youth.
Remain therein and tap His strength
And thus endure depth, breadth and length,
In dangerous day or distant move,
Sure of His presence and our strong love.

The Simpich Store

My entrance here is marked with memories
Of handmade marionettes alive on stage
Extolling timeless virtues to the young
In classic tales that shine more pure with age.

Escape to this bright world for just awhile.
Sit down, reflect, direct your weary eye
To images of humor, warmth and love,
Reviving childhood fancy with a sigh.

Quaint carolers, Abe Lincoln, Tom and Huck,
The Polar Friends, Cloud Babies with soft wings;
A humble Santa bows to Heaven's Babe
And teaches us th'eternity of things.

A family touch inspires the careful craft,
These miracles of plastic, cloth and wood.
They merit our endowment and we vow
A celebration of life under God.

[the Simpich Character Dolls store is in Colorado Springs, CO]

Proud When You Pass By

[upon Garrett's graduation from boot camp]

As you passed by in review
I was very proud of you.
Same fine son you've always been,
Tempered by harsh discipline.

Studded grip and powerful pull,
Mastery of principle.
Focus sharp and vision keen,
Poised and proper, long and lean.

More than man of self-defense,
Character and confidence.
Quintessential Semper Fi,
Unalloyed humility.

Virtue twinkles in your eye.
Timeless traits that God would try
Shining 'neath an azure sky
Make me proud when you pass by!

Three Things I have Learned from Striving

Three things I have learned from striving
As the hopeful father of three sons.
A bit of each, success and failure mixed–
Reflectively, I offer them to you,
Though not as having done them all, or well.

In the home teach timeless Book truth.
Do not leave this mission to the church -
Lest they think the expansive ways of God
Do not pervade each province of our lives.

Live and lead by quiet example,
Aligning spoken words and deeds performed.
Oh this, my sad shortcoming, sore defect!

Keep on praying, daily praying -
A better parent for the prayers, transformed.

For only God can Father and not fail.

Grow Old With Me

[written circa 1995]

I thank God for the wife he gave,
But even more, the woman you've become.
We reveled, frolicked in the springtime joy
Of nurturing the garden that was home.

We bravely faced hot summer days,
And over you this demon illness crept.
You take health hardships with such noble grace,
It merits my profoundest deep respect.

Now, colored leaves adorn the path;
It is a bright fall day, among our best.
You shall endure, the queen of my domain;
Meanwhile, we renovate the vacant nest.

Fanning embers of parent passion,
Let love and youth and newness enter in.
Our house may be the den of playful noise,
Our pride, the legacy of three young men.

Grow old with me! I pray and plead
With God, fount of all longing, all desire.
This is my crystal vision, only dream,
One earthen hope that sets my soul afire.

For, slowly to our winter lives,
The Master of the seasons bids us come.
I set my strength to warm your lovely heart
As we tramp onward to that fairer home.

And wintry splendors, known to us
Grow more enchanting as we two shall see.
My love, we'll breathe the icy robust air
And still adore the frosted, leafless tree.

Daily Prayer for Deb

Every day
While I'm away
This promise upon you I pray
God's blessing and keeping
His gracious face shining
His Presence and peace
[Numbers 6:22-27]

Wanderer

[to Mike]

You set your face like flint – long roads await!
I see it in your eyes, the way you tend;
Your yearning for the journey, not its end
Alerts your sight, anoints your steady gait.

So street-wise, thrifty, daring, happy, strong,
Even the cold night, or a hungry day
Do not deter your vagabond desire;
You step into deep mist with but a song.

And know that where you wander, there go I.

I do applaud your back-to-simple style;
While others boast of minimums, you live them.
See those bereft of bread or gloves, you give them,
Save just enough to get you one more mile.

I know remorse for my part in your pain.
Know I am hurting too, though healed by Grace,
The grace I wish for you, the radiant Face
Of Him whose presence guards you in the rain.

And know that where you wander, there goes He.

The prodigal, he left his house to roam
From selfishness, but not so, you, my son.
Your search is worthy, healthy, it is done,
As one heart seeking for its haven-home.

When lonely, lay you down your travel staff;
Return your mother's tender love in kind
With just a note or call to ease her mind;
Daily and bold, her prayers on your behalf.

And know that where you wander, there goes she.

I love your searching, pray your search will lead
To Jesus' feet, where early it began,
And in the arms of Love, to Whom you ran
When you were but a boy with life ahead.

I miss your laughter, yet it shall return
For sure when you show up and ring the bell
Sporting a copper tan, with tales to tell,
Pictures to show and ways for us to learn.

And when the wandering's over, there go we!

Wounded Warriors

My three bright boys are very much like me-
Hurting and healing, hopeful, weak and strong.
Did I in pride or anger cause the wound,
Which cut their tender hearts when they were young?

My father fashioned me, I mark his steps;
He was the man, I am his progeny.
As generations race and not relent
I pass along his timid legacy.

My father's father was my youthful joy,
Yet he was grieving too; dark wounds he had,
Deep scars from his own battles, his defeats
Revealed in the deficiencies of Dad.

And so we trace ourselves back to the garden
Where early on the poison deftly spread.
Now dead and dying, blindly we give way
Unto the failures of our federal head.

Good men, we have been robbed of our birthright;
The trumpet sounds, hear, hear the reverie.
Rise up, reclaim the heritage of God
To be the men that we are meant to be.

As Adam's errant sons for whom Christ died,
Stop running, stand and strike; the battle rages!
Here set we the example for our sons;
We will not shirk the conflict of the ages.

For Billy
(I Wish for You Your Dream)

I wish for you your dream,
That dream that shakes and wakes you in the night
And sparks within you passion to perform.

To drive us, make us thrive,
Survive that we may keep our dreams alive,
The One who never sleeps gives us our dreams.

I've watched you grow, I love you so.
Your guitar music dream is also mine!
But you have far surpassed, the future waits.

I do affirm your dream!
But ask, would you accept a different dream,
The one God has for you?

I would you lived the dream
And living, give to others as you may.
You have such talent! Surely, what a gift.

I wish for you your dream.
All this, but most of all the special dream
That God who gives us dreams has dreamed for you

A Flower from Alabama

Today I drove across state lines
Between appointments on the way
Buoyed up by all your faithful prayers-
It was a safe, successful day.

But in the room my heart raced back
To where you sit wan, weak and wired,
And I returned a fervent plea
For strength and peace as you retired.

If we could wander hand in hand.
You would see land you've never seen;
The Hudson River, Georgia pines,
And bright orange flowers, profuse in Alabama.

I've viewed the sights and roamed the states
And savored meals on different plates.
And though I heed the commerce call
You are the sweetest sight of all.

The sturdy grip will soon release;
Endure the season patiently.
Until the day my travels cease,
I'll bring to you a flower from Alabama.

At Home in Rye

Alder bush and acorn, sagebrush, stream,
Land much like in paintings, or a dream;
Full of nature's therapeutic noise
And playful sounds of growing girls and boys.
Pristine paths trodden by cattle and game
Wind through woods that bear Creator's name.
Soft guitar chords on cool mountain air -
E'en without them, there is music there.
This pleasant home is by our Father given,
Enchanting all, but a mere glimpse of Heaven.

Chapter 4

Haiku

Haiku: a Japanese lyric verse form having three
unrhymed lines of five, seven and five syllables,
traditionally invoking an aspect of nature or the
seasons; a poem written in this form.

*[Some of these are a slight departure from the content, but not the
structure, of this revered art form]*

Misty flutes and curls
Rising from this cup of tea
Lost in ambient air

———

Big city asleep
Glimpses of a cobalt dawn
Big city awakes

———

Spices, hot and bold
Light the eyes, inflame the tongue
Love that salsa rush

———

Campers, tents, RV's
Proud upon the asphalt lot
A five star ghetto

———

Like Bach in Leipzig,
Mozart in Old Vienna -
In my element

———

Came a floweret bright
Beauty and simplicity
Precious, our Mae Lee

———

Flight in the balance
Thrust and lift meet gravity
Jumbo jet takes off

———

Once you find the truth
Embrace, proclaim, yet beware
Pride comes creeping in

———

Like a blazing light
Bursting through thin ragged veil
Truth through error shines

———

Rising fiery moon
Flashes 'cross the alpine lake
Campsite on the hill

———

They would bring me down
Many unnamed enemies
Standing on my Rock

———

Blue lupine, white lace
Carpet lands, line forest paths
Russian fields and woods

———

Many flimsy parts
Strengthened in coherent whole
Modular design

———

Living on high ground
Helps protect one from the floods
Of discouragement

———

Daily visitor
Flits from feeder back to tree
Neck like blinking strobe

Grey Pacific day
Sheen of dolphins showed to me
Truest ocean hues

———

Orange, red autumn leaves
Strewn along fall forest paths
Ordered, not random.

———

Flying in a V
Pattern of community
Winged Canadians

Unity of Three
Father, Son, Holy Spirit
Trinity of God

———

Breathless, we behold
Like kids in a candy store
Vagaries of God

———

Diamond facets, bright
Glints and gleams, reflected light
Perfections of God

Chapter 5

Song of Brokenness

Broken

Broken,
But not beyond the power of soul healing;
God's great and gracious scheme to me revealing
A holy character to emulate.
Faith's foundation holds.

Heartache,
But not the pangs of infidelity,
Transgression's harvest working upon me,
All born of selfish and short-sighted ways.
Heart still trusts and loves.

Crying,
But not the bitter tears of sad remorse
Over a wicked, wisdom-spurning choice,
Or disregarding conscience inner voice;
Tears mix pain with joy.

No presumption.
Direct this musing not toward man, but Him
To Whom for all His work high praise I send.
His glory and my growth its blessed end;
My suffering His love-labor.

Riding the Wave

Riding the wave of my recent success,
Thinking this is how God always should bless.
Wind at my back, direction clear,
Borne on by momentum, need only to steer,
Forgetting the crucible I have been through,
I forget there are those for whom these trials are new.
Health, wealth and prosperity -
It's a lie to think that's how it always will be.
Some things come easy, fall right into place.
Sometimes you walk with the wind in your face.
Waves of success, waves of suffering -
Our response is an offering.
Like the tide, waves come and go;
Good times, bad times ebb and flow.
Think not your measure of misfortune odd,
But at the hand of a loving God,
One who has suffered beyond what we know,
Who knows what we need both to learn and to grow.
Conforming to Jesus is suffering's end.
Ride this short wave holding onto His hand.

Cycles of Our Lives

Tonight the full moon lit a cloudless sky
So bright that Sagittarius was pale,
And Scorpio was blinded by its light.
When it is absent both shine big and bright.

So are the various cycles of the heavens;
The moon will wax and wane, full, quarter, new,
Obscuring constellations in its line.
Sometimes they shy away, sometimes they shine.

Today I read your letter, sad account
Of circumstances out of your control -
Delay, a setback, thwarted plans, some pain.
My sympathetic heart welled up again.

So are the various cycles of our lives;
The stream flows not unlike the heavenly one.
Small eddies at the edge do not impede
The progress and direction, nor the speed.

God's ways are as well ordered and as sure
As are the pathways of celestial lights.
A rising moon that makes the stars seem dim
Is no unplanned phenomenon to Him.

I Play That Game Well

Quote the creed and sound sincere,
Offer tithe but with no cheer,
Worshipping, but no joy here;
I play that game well.

Talk of close community,
Boast of Christian unity,
But, come trials, no help from me;
I play that game well.

Say that I will pray for you,
Never pray, but say I do,
Start to pray and not pray through;
I play that game well.

Play the church game, fill the role,
Make them think me pure in soul,
Hide hypocrisy's heart whole;
I play that game well.

Teach the Bible, read the Word,
Love men's praise when it is heard,
Self deceived but self-assured;
I play that game well.

Holy Father, grant new start.
Loving Savior, touch my heart!
Precious Spirit, do your part;
Cleanse each trace of hell.

Would that all may see the Son
As this race is daily run.
May I hear Your kind "Well done."
Grace has made me well!

Paradox of Joy

How shall we tell the paradox of joy?
Like bright buds blooming in a bed of weeds,
Tall, golden wheat-fields born of dying seeds.

Take and give comfort from the Comforter.
Past pangs endured, you bolster others now;
And weep with weepers, wipe angst ridden brow.

With laughers, laugh, and share a sweeter day.
Harsh bitter blows brought hard-won victory,
And chiseled holy features others see.

Get grace to sing and strength in spite of strain.
Take fleeting happiness or lasting joy?
The one time tarnished, one without alloy.

In gravity of crisis learn anew
The mystery that joy may come from pain,
The certain hope that peace will come again.

Man in a coma gripping daughter's hand-
See this and you begin to understand
The paradox of joy.

Saints Well Fed

The saints are well fed, fat, about to burst.
We soak it in and satiate ourselves
With concerts, dinners, teas and conferences,
Leagues, clubs, committees and societies.

Meanwhile brethren in foreign fields are faint,
Hard pressed and ill endowed, they struggle on
Rejoicing, faithful, making much of little,
While we, lethargic, yawn and sleep it off.

One dusty Bible page upon our shelves,
One penny from our coffers, glutted, full,
One castoff from our capital funds drive,
One dish leftover from our pot-luck feast

Would fill them, charge them, marshal their resolve,
Would see its use far stretched to meet their need,
Would strengthen them to serve and persevere
And multiply much fruit of small seed born.

We feast on hearing, knowledge, application
From worship, teaching, preaching, singing, greeting
And talking about praying more than praying.
Could it be true we need not more, but less?

[Postscript]

Forgive me, Father and forgive me, friends
If I exaggerate to make a point.
I am so very blessed, how shall I bless?
I am so full, so fat; whom shall I feed?

The Wall Between Us

Imposing and enduring, tall and wide,
This wall between us you and I have built.
Forbidding us to view each other's soul,
It rises steady, stretching side to side.

We have no site plan, only sharp-edged tools
That whistle as they glide across each plane.
You are the unwitting hod carrier
And I, the master mason with my rules.

We raise it brick by brick, rows upon rows.
The mortar, strong emotions and harsh words,
Pliant at first, then setting hard as stone.
The project is not plumb and yet it grows.

A barrier to isolate, divide;
The process, painstaking and purposeful.
Sometimes we switch our roles, but the result
Remains - a wall to separate and hide.

How can we raze this structure and begin
To reconstruct an edifice of love
Upon the old foundation, rugged still,
With windows open to refreshing wind?

Chapter 6

In Memoriam

[tributes to those who died, or have died since the verses were written]

This Tiny Life

Who knows the impact of a life,
The course that it will take?
A babe was born, then fell asleep
In altered rapture to awake.

The life was short and bittersweet;
It mingled pain with joy.
To get such love then let it go
Takes fire-tried faith without alloy.

His name was Nicholas, and the import
Of his earthly stay
Is told in terms of sanctity,
Not length of years or even day.

So soon will we resume the pace
And trust in God alone
Whose sovereign purposes are hid
But later on will be made known.

He could not speak or see or move
But heard a clarion call.
Five minutes was a lifetime;
This tiny life has moved us all.

For Kate

Like Job, you may not understand
Calamities at God's own hand.
Yet trust in spite of seeming strand
That your Redeemer lives.

Like David pray for willing spirit,
And know your blessed Lord will hear it.
By winsome faith His presence merit;
Doubt not the strength He gives.

Like Paul, feel His sufficient grace,
That floods your soul and lifts your face,
And rest in Jesus fond embrace;
Bright hope bears and believes.

Like Esther, for such time as this,
Bow to His will, what 'ere it is.
His strength is perfect, naught amiss;
The outcome He conceives.

You share in Jesus' suffering,
But shall arise on healing wing,
As over you the angels sing,
And tapestry He weaves.

Like loving saints, we hold you up
As we cry, Father, let this cup
Pass from our dear one, lift her up;
The Spirit intercedes and grieves.

Like all the heroes of the faith
Unburdened, set like flint your face
Prepare to run this grueling race
Young hero, Christ receives!

[Matt Engler and his new bride, Laura traveled with our choir to Ukraine to perform in churches, orphanages, schools, etc. Matt reached out to me and helped to ease the jitters of my first overseas trip. He was a joy to know and seemed to relate well with the Eastern European folk. Not long after our trip Matt was killed in an automobile accident. Laura, his wife of only a few months, was pregnant. The choir sang at Matt's memorial service.]

We Sang Through Tears

We sang through tears,
In halting mezzo forte harmonies
To foreign faithful, moved by their sad plight,
With Matt, whose heart reflected their delight.
And they were tears of love.

We sang through tears,
In awe of such commitment and such faith
That they would pledge with us to carry on,
With Matt, whose smile assured them we were one.
And they were tears of peace.

We sing through tears,
For Laura, with her embryonic joy,
We crush our doubts with hope that will not fail;
For Matt, whose spirit waits beyond the veil.
And they are tears of faith.

We sing through tears,
Take courage in time-tested promises,
And vow to finish what we have begun.
And Matt, whose soul is settled in the Son
Will know our tears of joy.

Chapter 7

Poems Mother Wrote

The poetry of Elizabeth Marshall Thompson has been published in a variety of newspapers and magazines. I am sure I got my admiration of the classics (music, literature, even movies) from her. I remember one late night as a teen, sitting up with Mom reading limericks together when everyone else was asleep. Just Mom and me.

Reflecting the loves, longings, struggles and humor of an intelligent and creative at-home mother in the 1950's and 1960's, this verse is reminiscent of those times in America. If you know something about poetry you may spot in Mom's poems a bit of the genius of Emily Dickenson. Mom, what a great job you did raising us! I love you.

Richard

My wife sent me to the super mart
A quart of milk to buy,
But on the way to the milk stand
The baked goods caught my eye.

A jelly roll, a raisin loaf,
A pie with cherries gay.
I put them in my basket and
Continued on my way.

I passed along the meat stand;
My eager eye did fall
On jars of Polish sausage
In sizes short and tall.

And there below the stewing meat
My joyous taste buds cried -
A standing rib roast perfect
With juices deep inside!

Oh, ever did a rib roast sweet
Seduce with flavor fine!
And there beyond the meat stand
Stood the shelf of cooking wine.

Along a wall of crackers stacked
With many a good variety
I picked a few, you need them when
You entertain society.

Next to crackers, man alive!
Were cookies stacked in rows.
A hundred kinds to choose from;
With trembling tongue I chose.

The chunks of cheese I next beheld.
My head I lost completely
In reds of some, and cheddar fair,
And longhorn mild and sweetly.

My wandering basket then did pause
In front of pickled peppers
And olives stuffed with almonds rare,
And artichokes and kippers,

Anchovies canned, sardines in oil;
My stomach all aflutter,
I found along the bottom shelf
Great jars of peanut butter.

I'd made the rounds, and near the door
The household goods display
Did lure me with its many things,
Gay plastic cups, and tray,

A ball of twine, a casserole,
A thing to sharpen knives,
A pair of pads to sit things hot,
A block for chopping chives.

My envy soared for housewives who
On market day can go
And in this magic pirate's cave
Of riches spend their dough.

I wondered as I paid my bill,
What is it brought me here?
A beverage of sorts, I think –
I'd better get some beer.

The Oldest Man I Know

The oldest man I know
Has just turned fifty-eight.
His rheumy old-eyes glow
With everlasting hate.

You daren't cross his lawn
To go collect his tariff
Or any other thing, because
He'll call the county sheriff.

He suffers from a ticky heart
Colds, chilblains, ulcers, croup,
Arthritis, rheumatism, cramps,
Pinched colon, hernia, droop.

His teeth contain old metal,
His hair a nest of nits,
He wheezes like a kettle,
He has a boil on where he sits.

I don't know if he's mean because he's sick
Or if he's sick because he's mean,
But I know he is the sickest, meanest
Man I've ever seen.

Making Do

Once a woman, dressed for church
Was missing one white glove.
She looked about and underneath
As well as up above.
Her only other gloves were red
And only white would do.
She couldn't change her outfit -
Time was of the essence, too.

A sudden thought appeared,
Above her head a light bulb shone:
"I'll wear the one I have," she thought.
"It'll have to do alone."

After church she met three members
She'd never met before
And everyone thought her very nice
And wanted to know her more

Because her ungloved handshakes
Were a sudden grand sensation
And it seemed to her she shook the hand
Of the entire congregation.

Lanier's Song

I like to walk where no man walks,
Where no man walks but me.
I like to be the first to see
A river, bush or tree.

I like the quiet and the diet
Of berries wild and tangy,
The heated pall, the waterfall
That echoes deep and twangy.

The squirrel's rustle, the river's mussel.
I track along the sand
Of river's edge, the muddy ledge
And dig him with my hand.

When I am free I plan to be
The pilot of a raft.
Alone I'll float my makeshift boat
With trotlines side and aft.

My lonely camp, though dry or damp
Will be my favorite haunt,
For I'm akin to fur or fin
And love a woodsy jaunt.

Watching a Symphony Orchestra Perform

The violin bows like slants of rain
      Pour out their liquid fulsome tones;
      The brass of trumpets and trombones
Repeat a softly sad refrain.

Come in the oboes rich as grain,
      And sweet melodious dance the flutes
      Bespeaking heavenly angels' lutes
Embellishing the celestial plain.

Conductor wildly waves baton
      Then coyly stills it, beckons, pleads,
      Now stabs and jabs, now calmly leads;
His dripping forehead lock curls on.

The horns echo medieval tone
      Supported by the deep bassoon
      With tympani punctuated tune
And cello's and base viol's drone.

At last the mighty winds and strings
      Proclaim in chorus the grand finale.
      Shouting cheers, applause, and rally;
Encore! Encore! Encore! rings.

Laggard Moon

Trapped in the chimney smoke
And about to be sliced in two
By that jagged mountain peak,
Knife-sharp and metal-cold,
With all that snow,
Night watchman
That hates to leave
Until the sun takes over---
Where were you that day
The sun didn't show up at all?

Mountain Storm

The shameless shimmy of the fir,
Most graceful of the trees;
The pines upon the distant hill
Obscured by misty breeze;
No shadows on the landscape dim;
One shadow over all,
As mountains crouched beneath their veil
Peek shyly through the fall.
A watercolor scene is this,
Washed over by the torrent's kiss.

After a False Spring

I went along the snowy hedge;
The startled robins left the ledges
Where frozen cascades in the stream
Had caught and held the crumbs and seeds
And icy pearls held down the weeds.
I'd wished that spring were here to stay,
That green would take the place of grey.
But can I disappointed be
To see a countryside that's so
Serene and richly dressed in snow?

A Very Old Couple in Church

Such a very old couple,
From behind she looks like his little brother
And his head, like a baby chick newly sprung
From its white, white shell.

Such a snow-white, exceedingly pale pair,
Fragile father, delicate mother
Sitting while the standing hymns are sung
After the fire and brimstone yell.

A peaceable, unafraid couple,
They seem to feel they can go no farther;
Appraise the past and what's to come
In onrushing swell.

Black-and-white-clad white-haired folks
Sitting at the end of the polished pew;
Quiet as china dolls on a shelf,
Fine as crystal bells.

Chapter 8

Song of Mission

In 1998 the Bear Valley Church choir traveled to
Ukraine to perform sacred concerts. We did the same
in 2001, this time to Moscow and the surrounding
areas. Those were days when the fall of Communism
was fresh in our memories; both countries were
experiencing a new era of openness and upstart
churches were flourishing. These poems reflect
impressions from both trips.

Losing Weight in the Land of Plenty

Strolling
Supermarket rows,
(Doc said,
"Many pounds to lose"),
Primed to visit
The Ukraine,
Losing now to later gain,
As I scanned this lavish sight
I began to see the light.
Seeming sea of blood red meat,
Some prepared, some, cook to eat.
Every kind of bottled juice, painter's palette of produce
Watered even as it waits, home to go, steamed, fill our plates.
Fish and poultry, sausage, hams, rows and rows of colored cans,
Packs of pasta, white, green, red, racks and racks of fresh baked
bread,
Freezers full of rich ice cream, each an epicurean dream.
As I learn to read the stats, carbs and saturated fats,
Proteins, fiber, vitamins, rue my culinary sins-
Deli salads, readymade, milk and cheeses, all A grade,
Miles of artificial light, air-conditioned day and night.
No surprise to see so many heavy in the land of plenty!
How can I control, resist, tempted by such fare as this?
Maybe when I leave to fly
To that land
Of sparse supply
And   consume
Their meager   share, pounds
won't be my   problem, there.

Monuments to Majesty

Spiritual corruption,
Social disruption,
Church construction;
Foundations fast.

Monuments to Majesty,
Structural integrity,
Functional simplicity;
Built to last.

Blood of martyrs,
Sweat of members,
Tears, prayer warriors;
Building on the past.

Refiner's cauldron,
Molding children,
Childrens' children;
Hope is cast.

Windows to heaven,
Strong spikes driven,
New leaven;
Torch is passed.

Meet Me at the Throne of Grace

As I am so far away,
You are in my thoughts today.
Let us trust our sovereign Lord;
Where you are, kneel down to pray.

I will travel to His throne
While I pray for you alone.
Jesus bids us meet Him there,
Make our distant longings known.

I am on this mission, dear,
Reasons not completely clear.
Thank you for your sacrifice;
God will bless you while I'm here.

Though you can't be in this place
You can seek His loving face.
Hand in hand we'll travel there
To the Father's throne of grace!

What a joy to know that we,
Praying, can together be.
We are really two made one,
Separated by the sea.

Long Before the Fall

How long can you live a myth,
Perpetuate a lie?
Ill advised designs go bad
And evil schemes, awry.

Cold war propaganda
Touted modern streets
And modern high rise buildings
And large industrial feats.

We believed the system
Inspired fear and awe;
But we traveled silent,
Stunned by what we saw.

Farmlands lying fallow,
Plants in ill repair,
Unsafe streets and buildings
Ruin far and near.

Lest you think this happened
In a brief bad time,
Evidence shows decades
Of recession and decline.

Oppression of the people,
Deficiency of health,
Crime and wealth, a vile elite,
Persecuted faith.

Slowly but foreboding,
Hidden from us all,
Was Communism's crumble
Long before the fall.

Moment of Truth

As I observe the faithful of this realm
Face hardship and harsh circumstance with joy,
I comprehend the Church of Christ will stand
Against the winds of change in any land.

And when will my own testing time arrive?
Or has it, unbeknownst, already come?
What is this faith I casually profess?
False? Or a true fire-tested holiness?

Would I deny my Master on that day?
And, like sad Peter, say "I know Him not?"
Or dare I shrink from persecution's threat?
My fear of failure undiminished yet!

This peoples' hearts are steadfast with resolve.
Lord Jesus said, "The spirit wills, flesh wanes."
Therefore are we compelled to watch and pray
And don Paul's perfect armor every day.

So if my part is death or life to serve,
God will adjudge, and if I fail, forgive.
The outcome was resolved, to my relief
The hour my heart awakened to belief.

Ukrainian Children

Hidden treasure beneath the Trident sign,
The country's future, full of promise, bright -
Ukrainian children, precious, golden gifts,
Their hearts wide open to a pure new light.

Their smiles belie the long and obvious strain
Of every parent's hard-bitten countenance
Their public manners all above reproach,
The fruit of careful household governance.

So playful, innocent, eyes full of fun,
They rush to thank you for a simple toy.
Without presumption, how they laugh and run,
And weep when a newfound friend waves goodbye.

They fill my memory and I am undone.
God loves them all – and also loves each one.

Tale of Two Orphans

Two little children, one a blond,
The other with red hair,
From shattered, heart-sick families,
No home or comfort there.

One orphanage, state-run,
The other by believer's purse
The contrast is unspeakable,
Between the care and curse.

Two motives, one an obligation,
One love's labor pure,
Two warring world-views beget
And raise their offspring sure.

A dismal prospect for the one,
For other, rays of hope,
Two destinies, two lives at risk,
The magnitude and scope!

The tale is not fully told;
It waits for time and strife.
We wonder how a youth so reared
Could rise and conquer life.

One sovereign God Who knows each soul
And all the secret harms,
Please place them under Your right, strong
And everlasting arms.

A Holy Moment

Ring of truth in a foreign land,
The bell choir was in Cyndie's hand.
Through the morning she had fought
To hold back tears, but all for naught
As she beheld the children come,
An orphanage, their spartan home.
This was a holy moment.

Tonight, her tired, angelic face
Reflected Jesus' joy and grace.
As we prepared to share the Word
With songs and bells, a noise was heard.
They played, "Give Thanks with a Grateful Heart."
What Cyndie sensed gave her a start.
This was a holy moment.

The folk began to hum along,
Surprised that they should know the song.
Ukrainians and state side singers
Accompanied by glad bell ringers
United hearts in one accord
To hum soft praises to the Lord.
This was a holy moment.

Moon Over Donetsk

From the balcony of my room
The last night of my stay,
I view the falling crescent moon
Going, like me, away.

Brilliant, bright-arched sliver
Crown jewel of the star studded sky –
I pause and form a metaphor,
I pray and ponder why.

Resemblance of hammer and sickle
Recalls a former day –
Once a leering symbol,
Now icon of decay.

God of mercy, miraculous
The entrance of gospel light!
Grant this land a glad new day
Beyond the moonlit night.

Precious Faith

Returning from that vast and distant land
I ponder the adventures of two weeks
Of joyful service and of lessons learned
In concert with the joyful, hearty band.

I had already learned contentment's home
Before I saw firsthand their abject want.
I had already known my share of pain
Apportioned by God's hand, as is their own.

So what was gained while visiting this place?
In truth, I traveled just to find it out.
I found what I had sought and ample more –
The answer's in the people and their faith.

I saw it in their faces, joyful gleam
Of eyes hemmed in by lines of hardship, hurt,
A stern resolve to press on, faithful, strong,
An understated smile with holy beam.

I heard it in their praises, how they sing!
An ardent passion, come from hearts enlarged;
Restrained but deeply felt, their kind response,
Sincere and loving tones sung to the King.

I felt in their places, worship halls –
Those giant stately beams and rising roofs!
I sensed the hand-made bricks could speak trust-tales
One purpose as they build and break down walls.

I learned to fear not harsh adversity,
Of self submissive to the holy cause.
Fear not a bold abandonment but fear
The hellish quagmire of complacency.

Once for all time delivered to the saints,
Our faith is precious, purchased with the blood
Not only of God's Son, but those whose lives
Courageously embodied all His pains.

Together, we've a saintly sideline crowd
That bids us be steadfast, unmovable,
Abounding, vigorous in love's strong deeds,
Illuminating all the grace of God.

In Russia with Love

Awesome God, we firmly stand,
Stand to sing and ring your praises
In this once forbidden land.

God of mercy, grant us grace,
Grace to go where mercy sends us,
There to seek and shine Your face.

Faithful One, our hearts are fixed,
Fixed upon the task before us,
Faithful, fearful feelings mixed.

Ringing "Holy, Holy, Holy,"
Giving "Thanks with a Grateful Heart,"
"Wondrous Love" and "Majesty."

Father, fainting, weary, weak,
Weak but winging on your strength,
In your name we sing and speak.

Singing, "So you Would Know,"
"Knowing You" and "He Is Risen,
Hallelujah," universal word.

Young Men of Mozhisk

Prison pallor pressed us down
As we drove up the lanes
And saw gaunt faces peering
From behind cracked windowpanes.

The razor wired stronghold
Housed a hellish black despair
Of stark, stern-handed discipline;
No love or comfort there.

We sensed thick clouds of strong oppression,
Raging demon wars.
But when we prayed the locks fell off,
And we passed through the doors.

And there we faced them, strong young men,
High foreheads, deep-set eyes,
Hard chiseled features, long and lean,
Beneath warm Russian skies.

They thought their jeers and smiles could hide
Their pain from our purview.
But holy music broke the cloud
And Sonlight filtered through.

Erin with her radiant smile,
Bernadine who signed,
Norma at the violin
Brought Wondrous Love to mind.

Dane, who spoke of thieves and choices,
Scott who sought to intercede
Alice backed by bells and voices
Sowing truth as gospel seed

We are not the reapers now;
Be patient through the years.
But we shall seek the Harvest Lord,
And water prayers with tears.

Bells of Suzdal

Assorted bells, once melted into cannon;
Long since replaced, they ring each day at three.
Sublime and seasoned tones like angels float
'Cross copula skyline of old Suzdal.
Kliasma wends its calm pastoral way
Where tourists wander, ponder, zoom and shoot
And cattle graze and children fish and play.

'Twas here we came to give, but were denied
And made instead to listen, look, receive.
And while the bright bell thunder peals and rolls
O'er ancient towers and monastery walls,
It bids arousal of past mystic shades
Of merchants, monks, peasants landed and poor
Who plied their secular and sacred trades.

Male voices, like a well-tuned string quintet
Intone the doleful music of high church.
Their notes reverberate off frescoed walls
To caption colors, epic Scripture scenes.
Such heavenly harmonic reveries laud,
Such quaint beauty ensconced in history
Bespeaks deep yearning for the love of God!

I ask my longing heart, what is this place?
Bold, dome-flecked landscape,
Live with songs of faith?
(On my own life, I wish it so!)
Or Orthodoxy's bastion, bland or dead?
(I fear the worst, yet hold to hope)
Transcendent God, yet by Christ known to us,
Revive this weary land within our scope!

And while the bright bell thunder peals and rolls,
Grant grace, pour peace upon sad Russian sou**ls.**

Potter's Wheel

Now I know what Jeremiah saw.
To potter's place God sent him,
And bade him watch and learn.
The potter throws the shapeless wet,
Sometimes defiant or passive, pliant lump
Upon the moving circle, there to be turned and
Worked. His fast feet work the wheel, his hands,
The clay upon the wheel. With strong, lithe hands
And ah, deft fingers he applies water and pressure,
Smooth palms and fingertips, using water well.
The thing changes as it grows; he fashions
For beauty and utility. Shape secure,
But then endures sharp and sudden
Separation from the wheel, entry
Into the oven for fiery trial.
But not to fear; the vase,
Made for this. Result,
Only the potter knew.
It exits a seasoned,
Vessel of honor.
The outcome was
Sure. Unknown to me,
But not the potter. The changes
May surprise all who see, but not the potter.
The picture prompts a plea - Oh Christ, be formed in me!

Meet Me in Red Square

Celebrate the times with me
Along the cobbled way;
Kingdoms crumbled, saintly prayers
Brought Jesus back to stay.

Hit the shops and kiosks
Buy trinkets, dolls and lace.
Reconvene by Lenin's tomb
(Handy meeting place).

Change your money, translate words,
Find that friends are here.
Interact with lovely folks
That we were taught to fear.

Snapshots at the base of Basil's
Shopping in the Gum,
Near the man's memorial,
Tower clock strikes noon.

Walk where missiles, tanks and troops
Were fearsome on display.
By the dead man's brittle bones
Let us stop and pray.

Stroll along the Kremlin walls,
Ponder world events.
Pass the fallen leader's grave
And give a passing glance.

View along the marble bridge
River's winding ways.
Gather back at great Red Square,
There we'll sing God's praise!

Speak Through Me

Lord, what do you wish to say
Through this cracked and breaking, seeping
Pot of unglazed clay?

Grace that deigns to speak through me,
Uninspired earth utensil,
Sinful though I be!

Blood of Christ spilt, stop the leaking,
Cleanse the vessel, flush and fill it –
Poured out, Spirit speaking.

Master, let me voice your will
Mouth your counsel, weak and shaking;
I, your servant still.

Chapter 9

Miscellany of Observes

*[wherein are offered various random thoughts,
notions and perspectives on many things]*

Some Pretty Good Double A Ball

National anthem sweetly sung
By a talented trio of senior girls.
Jump starts the contest, fresh legs run,
Strategic mind game now unfurls.
Friendly subplot spirit bout
Between fans and rival cheerleading corps.
Sneaker squeaking intensity
Up and down the blue-gray tartan floors.

Average athletes form the teams,
Except two giants we applaud:
Number thirty-two, Ewert
Matched with Ponder on the opposing squad.
Senior lettermen, college bound,
Six-foot-four on six-foot-eight,
Scouting report on the marquee players,
Two of the best on the Double A slate.

Home team passes and dribbles well,
Jumpers, layups, zone, man-to-man.
Ebb and flow, momentum shift,
Twenty-point swing in an eight-minute span.
Girl in the bleachers four rows up,
Scream sounds like the referee's whistle.
Silly sophomore groupies mind
Themselves, not the game, and gray hairs bristle.

Home team, up by ten in the third,
Ends up losing by seven points.
Away we saunter down from the stands,
Loosening idly stiffened joints.
Supporting students, school and sport,
Pleased with the program overall,
Irked about the final score
But pleased with some pretty good Double A ball.

State Highway Nine

This road is less traveled than many I know.
I follow a rancher who drives the speed limit;
It seems, to me, slow.

I watch herds of Herefords and longhorns together
Along the barbed fence line with cavalier bearing;
Calm, late July weather.

The pastoral scene is a painter's perfection
With vast panoramas of snow capped peaks
In every direction.

Cloud formations conspire in collusion
Of sunshine and shadow upon rolling hills,
Wildflowers in profusion.

Serene scenic shortcut, State Highway Nine-
It starts near the Canyon and comes out at Hartsel.
Thanks for Your time.

Sneakers on the light pole-
How'd they get that high?
How long will they stay?
What do they imply?

The Homeless Person's Market Strategy

The market-savvy, street-wise vendors ply
In quick-time drive up window transactions
Their hand-to-mouth existence daily trade
At busy lack-shade city intersections.

Old cardboard seems the perfect medium,
Felt markers scroll the sappy sales pitch.
Though some still favor home delivery,
New studies validate this market niche.

Times change, and so consumer preferences.
Cost-benefit assumptions time will prove.
Creative slogans drive desire to buy.
Taglines invoke a blessing from above.

Entrepreneurship mixed with charity -
Suppliers drop off what they do arrange.
The demographic targets those who drive.
For service rendered, pay with pocket change.

They stand and stare, hold 'loft their dire theme
Along debris-strewn, weedy walk or off ramp,
Asleep to civic duty – blind it seems -
Cornered the market, but won't clean the camp.

All entry level opportunities.
All boundaries they recklessly define.
The only overheads – sun, clouds and sky.
All proceeds drop straight to the bottom line.

Point and Counterpoint

Point and counterpoint-
Agree to disagree agreeably.
A thesis, antithesis, synthesis
Framing the debate.

On Emily's Dejection (#747)

Whence came the deep – despondency -
And what, the hope misplaced?
What pain of disillusionment
With melancholy laced?

And, were they truly plated wares,
Or precious, misconstrued?
I pray you, was it mere pinchbeck
Or gold that she eschewed?

Kudzu

The creeping vine, it goes, it grows and slows
The erstwhile growth of other living things.
As under sheets fine furniture undiscerned,
That foreign force, unwelcome visitor
Misshapes the beauteous forms of things.
It blunts sharp edges and removes clear gaps
And generalizes stark particulars;
Arrogant blanket blocks the sun and saps
The life of plants and bushes, rustic fences,
Or like a market slogan masking, draping
Production defects or morale malaise.
Like kudzu o'er Georgia, you cover me;
Why must you smother, blithely mother me,
Think you must deign to hover over me?

He Who Travels Well

He who travels well
Leaves not a trace upon the land,
But imprints on each heart and every hand.

He who travels wisely
Remembers well from whence he came
And once again returns to speak the Name.

He who seeks the Spirit
Will know the signs on hills and shores,
Like cat paws, kitten purrs and Lion roars.

Comfort Food

Come now and let us reason together.
Aren't you making too much of comfort food?
Stop and ask yourself to consider whether
A food can really bring back your childhood?
Or make you feel better when you're sad?
Or in a flurry give a sense of peace,
Or calm your nerves when you are fighting mad?
Or help you gain a measure of release?
Food for the stomach, the stomach for food.
No sense in making more of it than this.
Just be thankful we have enough and good.
Three squares a day, then on to your business.
Now, time to start my day and make the most.
(And time to go fix my morning cheese toast…)

A Miscellany of Observes

Game show hosts are polished people;
Their contestants, too.

When young you wish for futures fast,
But for the aged, days rush by.

People doing what they love,
Finding joy in doing,
Seem most to succeed.

The event is not the thing;
Process matters most.

Modular design joins weak components
And makes one sturdy, strong, coherent whole.

Candles in church are an ancient custom;
Reverting back to them is postmodern.

To recognize the power of paradox
Is truest thinking outside of the box.

English is poetic! I mean,
We *speak* in iambic pentameter.

the Artist in me

at times I'm all locked up inside...
a secret gift – wrapped and ribboned.
or... yes! a bed of smoldering coals
wanting the Wind to fan me into flame.

ah, for a breath of fresh creative Breeze
to move again, blow gently over me,
and whoosh! a brief but brilliant fire-flash
to warm cold hearts and give new light.

come out, come out! reveal Yourself-
the only Fire that takes the form,
the ash, smell, smoke and cinder
of that which it consumes.

I shall not shrink, but gladly bear the burning.
the Artist in me is You.